# In the Telling

## GAIL ASHTON &
## SUSAN RICHARDSON (eds)

Published by Cinnamon Press
Meirion House
Glan yr afon
Tanygrisiau
Blaenau Ffestiniog
Gwynedd, LL41 3SU
www.cinnamonpress.com

The right of the contributors to be identified as author of this work has been asserted by them in accordance with the Copyright, Designs and Patent Act, 1988. © 2009
ISBN 978-1-905614-92-9
British Library Cataloguing in Publication Data. A CIP record for this book can be obtained from the British Library.

Designed and typeset in Palatino by Cinnamon Press
Cover design by Mike Fortune-Wood from original artwork, 'Darkness' by Nazira G. courtesy of dreamstime.com

Printed in Great Britain by the MPG Books Group,
Bodmin and King's Lynn

# Contents

## Beneath the Weave:

## Pulling the Thread:

## *Spindled:*

*What the Weaver Knows:*

# Foreword

When we put out the call for submissions to this anthology, we hoped to be surprised and intrigued by new versions of age-old folk and fairy tales, to be shaken and stirred by contemporary myths and urban stories, to listen to the voices of people past and present, as well as to the voices of places, landscapes and artefacts.

We weren't disappointed. Our email inboxes were soon vibrating to the snores of scores of Sleeping Beauties; awash with selkies, mermaids and Noahs; preyed on by packs of Red Riding Hood's wolves. There were comic poems, tales of personal and global disaster, stories of love between all kinds of different beings, from Glaswegian teenagers to green peas...

Across some four thousand poems, image after image was spun, woven, unbuckled, unwrapped to challenge our selection process and convince us that narrative poetry is currently thriving.

*Susan Richardson*

What inspired this collection of poems? - the certainty that between us and the rest of the world is only stories.

If we could know these stories, we would scent them trembling in open fields. Hear them dancing in a clash of edges. Feel them drawing through the chambers of our hearts. Listen. They knock at forbidden doors. They call to us in strange tongues, skin and bone. Taste of dreams, coral, cobalt. Not all of them are gorgeous or short of breath. Not all of them have a name. But regardless of their place of birth, they all have *mouths no-one can stitch shut* (Flaming Sue).

Listen. They are *talking through the language of things* to bring us together. They are how worlds drift in; are held at bay; open doors; fall through the weave. This book is one of those stories.

*Gail Ashton*

# In the Telling

*beneath the weave*

# Beneath the Weave

*Arlene Ang*

*There is a maiden, nurtured in the halls of Aeetes, whom the goddess Hecate taught to handle magic herbs with exceeding skill...*

Apollonius Rhodius, *Argonautica* 3.528

Her eyes have it: indigo smoke,
slow scythe of flesh, wine, crow's feet,
sometimes shipwreck underwater.

She enters silently, the way hemlock
sinks in a steaming cauldron.
In the torchlight, her hair is uncoiled.

The loom casts witch shadows
on walls. She hums, and poisoned flax
wounds around the distaff.

She is at the autumn of her crocus:
a nuptial robe for her husband's bride,
yew and monkshood in the mortar.

She spins rivulets of fire from
Phlegethon. The air glows; she is
ochre-lipped like approaching dawn.

This is how Medea walks away:
the palace burns around the wedding
banquet. Her secret is in the weave.

# Spillikins
Susan Morgan

*Human remains, dated 3700 BC*


A heap, did you say?
These bones are
high and dry,
wind and wood
knocking on wood.
You can almost hear
the protesting child
running from bed:
I don't want to go to sleep now!

Percussive, hollow
gamelan cry.

Strung up, they'd dance
with comical, loose
grins, before
collapsing in a heap;
arm-cradled,
kept in a basket
of lucky-bone charms.
Tell them your secrets;
they'll tell you your fortune.

Play an engrossing game
of crisscrossed spillikins.

# Mother Hubbard
Ann Walters


An old woman sitting on a step
tosses grains of rice carved from stone
to men in suits and urgent strides.

She hands paper ears of corn
to the children who call her Auntie
as they pass on their way to school
while their mothers get wooden chilies
enameled in red and orange,
or sweet straws of honey
shaped from clay and painted gold.

But for the wastrel dogs that lie
at her feet and thump their tails,
she has bones, plucked one by one
from her own withered frame
and offered without hesitation.

# A Lesser Deity

Mim Darlington

*Flora*

On the first day she drew the anatomy of her heart
and superimposed it upon a piece of overgrown wilderness

on the second day she wound the weeds round and round
herself so that the earth was bare and she was green

on the third day she walked over the naked soil
sewing a careful tapestry of seeds

on the fourth day she doused for springs
strengthened their outpouring with granite and rocks

on the fifth day she brought in children to plant soft fruits
and advise about lawns and hiding places

on the sixth day she did not rest because every woman knows
what happens if you take your eyes off something for a minute

on the seventh day earthworms, snails, insects, lizards
weasels and lovers came, followed by many birds

on that day, God made a surprise visit
and on his way out he left the gate open

and afterwards they found he had left his shoes.

# The Need to Get A Life
Helen Pizzey


In shops I linger over
needle-heeled crocodile,
finger soft pads of linings,
hum to the clatter of lids against boxes
and the hiss of pristine tissue.

On Fridays I take my pick
from outside mosques,
cuddle those lifted from
bouncy castles at weekends.

Even security at Heathrow
sometimes leaves at least
one traveller fretfully barefoot
on the far side of a screen.

Back home, my garage light
illuminates an Aladdin's cave of soles,
each neatly stowed and labelled
in its place on racks of shelving.

Here a treadmill rumbles on,
grumbling through the night;
measures lone miles walking
in another person's shoes.

# Lilith

Rosie Garland

He spent the day pointing at creatures and mumbling
stumbling on this new invention, words.
Eyes heavy clay like theirs; brows hauled together
when I stroked his arm.  Named me: *woman*.
Shook me off.
On his toes each evening when God walked
through the trees. I preferred to pick my teeth
after eating meat.  I still do.
I will not be two syllables rattling in his mouth.
I am half sand, and fall away if not held to my liking.

She gets as much of nothing as I did,
but lacks the skill to laugh and walk away.
Converses with serpents, listens to their promises
of makeup to cover the bruises, hides the toys
they bring her as if it makes a difference.
Bears the name he gave her, soon his cubs.
He whimpers when she touches him, clutches his side.

I braid my hair in snakes with fingers sugar sticky.
Hang necklaces of breasts beneath my chin.
Turn women to butter, men to stone.
When I dance, the sky drops water, the earth moans.

# New Crop

Tamara Madison


In spring the girls
wear their autumn romances—
September mistakes,
October lapses,
fleeting football game
infatuations—
like beach balls
beneath their babydoll
T-shirts.
Once a shame on the family,
grounds for a hasty wedding,
a ship-off to relatives
in a distant state,
now as common as DUI,
bankruptcy, divorce.
In clumps of girls they stand
fresh-faced, lovely
in this pause before
their lives change forever,
before they'll have
more in common
with their own mothers
than they now have
with these friends.
In nearby shadows
behind school buildings
clothed couples spend
whole lunchtimes joined
at hip and lip, as nearby
babies thunder
in the bellies of the girls
who now stand boyless
in the sun and incubate
a new crop of soldiers

# Swings and Roundabouts
Anne Caldwell


I'm in a hammock in the garden
clutching Alice Hoffman's latest novel,
the lawn burnt to a tinder.

You rise like a cry in my mind.
High pressure bursts.
A downpour washes leaves clean of dust.

My headache lifts like a red kite
and you're curled in your London flat
on a black sofa stuffed tight with feathers.

You had seven good eggs to choose from:
Hope had been a rising line of mercury in the heat.
Outside your window, tarmac bubbles,

The Capital's green lungs are
crammed with lovers. You text me.
*IVF failed. No joy this time.*

As kids, we tested our sense of balance
on the see-saw in Congleton park,
grey pleated skirts billowed like shuttlecocks:

one life up, one life down.
It's always been this way between us.
I got pregnant as simply as a jump from a swing.

You're thirty-nine, inject your stomach
till it blooms yellow, then purple.
Through the skylight, you watch a plane tree

flaming before winter desiccates the city.

# Medusa's Garden
Gabriel Griffin


On Italian lines, rather formal, spare,
exquisite topiary, the box and yews
clipped into shapes of beasts, though you might choose
to note that shining ponds and pools were rare—

no reflection, you understand, is there
on the late owner, who, with eyelids closed,
bemoaned the total lack of good coiffeurs
and how those snakes *would* get into her hair!

Those pretty boys who sometimes came her way
just stood there turned to stone; of them, not one
was bold enough to look into the eyes
and see the yearning there no words could say...

she'd sigh, admire the statuary alone.

# The Wild Swans

Marilyn Donovan

A ribboned lake. An early-morning flight
of swans wraiths round my tower
in sinuous loop, peels off in silence.
My brothers.

Eleven white feathers drift
through the bars.

This night was bitter as steel, still
save for my frantic hands. Silver
dandelion seeds  of stars hung frozen,
the stasis of a rocket burst before
its slow collapse towards rapt crowds below.

I sent the rat-tailed priest away.
What use the exhortation of one so keen
to smell out sin but blind to innocence?

Eddies of sound — the scrape and snap
of dragging wood, gruff instructions.
The witch.

Ten coats finished.
What care I for the burning in my feet,
blisters scalding hands and arms?
All night I trampled nettles, stripped
leaves, shredded stems to flax.
Now I weave, weave, weave.

Crowds clamour at the gate.
Already a blood-orange sun rises.

# Poplars on the Bank of the Epte
## Martin Willitts

*Based on the painting by Monet who paid the owner not to cut down the*
*poplars so he could make the painting.*

The poplars are mute. They know
I can no longer protect them.
Their leaves no longer rustle in
green whispers. There, at their ankles
were the pre-cutting, the incision
trying to hide behind a gauze of moss.

I paid the owner to spare them
so I could use this scene
knowing that when I was done
they would be gone so no one
could see they were removed
forgotten like the one legged soldier.

I move a flat stone for my composition
not pleased with its original location.
I noticed it is flint for scratching flame
for the soldier's pipe, then the gnarled knees
of the bark, the whiskers of bristled leaves,
the far hills in his cataracts and fragile light.
The trees became geometric rigor of his fingers.

So I paid to delay the land owner
sharpening his blade, mocking the waste of money,
knowing soon everything will fall, it is inevitable.

# Reading February
Trent Halliday


There's the crisp mounted field, folded, sled,
every blade-edge a crystal, a water cocoon.
I imagine them hatching butterflies, a swoon
of perfect blue armours rising from frozen beds.
I want to catch one and read their paper wings
wrap my lips round February's wise wet things.

There's the puddle-skin waking to a blackbird's
dip and trill, dowsing the white roadside
in a muddle of feet-crossed arrows and lines.
I imagine them forming pictures: branch-shards
chiselled from azure; engravings of a white dove.
I want to frame and hold them to my breast like love.

There's the scent of snowdrops dangling trinities
beneath the tree-palm's wrinkles and wire.
I imagine their tenor weaving through briar-thorns
entangled with the duplum of a primrose's melody.
I want to hear them, pick them from the old nylon
weave them into a song-bed for us to lie on.

# Heron
Ian Clarke

the dark thaws
to foxglove, balsam,
bracken's hooked and tender green,
to a river fish tickled

and dewpond fresh,
and where roots claw the bank
rain softens
to a cold smouldering,

and where winter fades
buried with bog-oak and bone,
the ghost of a gibbet
fogged and gallows still,

coming up for air.

# Women like Wolves

Marilyn Jenkins

*A tale of the poet Cas Corach*

Each night Artech's three daughters
hunt sheep at the Cairn
of Bricre. Wolf Women,
immune to human steel, leave
Cailte and his people helpless,
their only hope, the song of
Cas Corach their chief pleads:

*Cas Corach, singer of songs,*
*only you can melt them to earth*
*coax off their rough pelts, shape women*
*ripe for the spear. I Cailte*
*urge you—Save our lambs.* Again
with night, they come, explode
along their werewolf run to

the cairn where drifts of sound
from Cas Corach's lute beguiles
them . Entranced, they listen:
*I will see the beauty you*
*hide like a moon behind cloud .*
*I will see your soft mouths. Your*
*white hands, now veiled, reach out.*

Each night they return gentler.
Soon they lie with the lambs to
watch his lute fall, his lips move,

whisper: *closer, come closer,*
*only ears tuned to human*
*sound  can catch the full bliss*
*of my music—so, come, close,*
*still closer, come closer,*

*in line—come.* The moon shudders
off its clouds as beasts dissolve.
Skies lighten as three women
rise from the earth. The poet
sings without break, takes up
his spear, air gasps as he throws.

Flesh yields softly to wood. Cas
Corach sings as he strings the
necks of Artech's daughters like
trout on a pole. Three women
softly offer their blood to earth
in silence.

# The dreams of Briar Rose, the Sleeping Beauty

Rachel Mann


I blew forty years' worth getting blitzed on Special Brew,
dancing the meringue 'til my toes bled,
drinking debutantes under the table,
taking sweaty cabinet ministers (a bit of rough) to bed.
For fifteen years, I just wept—that 'finger prick disaster'
replaying, like a schlock horror movie, in my head,
the spinner woman, that old crone, morphing
between Xena Warrior Princess,
Queen Victoria, Hitler and Clark Kent;
I brained her with the sewing machine,
caused GBH with a telescopic mallet,
chinned her Glaswegian style, sliced her in half
with the Kung Fu Buddhist Palm.

Then again, I spent 5 happy years skiing
with Isambard Kingdom Brunel (bad hat),
invented 48 new varieties of jam,
ate pomegranates with God,
played Jane to Johnny Weissmuller's Tarzan.

And, of course, I dreamt of *him*:
tall, lean limbed, a footballer's arse,
blue-green eyes, tanned, olive skin.
He's worn Arab style drapes, buckled some swash in pirate togs,
occasionally bored for England in a Savile Row suit.
Once, he was my dad.

I woke to bed sores and an itchy back. A body floppy as a doll.
*Him* leering over me: my grinning saviour, blank eyed as a shark,
as pleased as a cat pinning down a sparrow. All teeth and bad breath.
I screamed for a month.

Doc says it's *post-excessive sleep syndrome*.
Mum and dad, at least, are glad: Aubrey has just the right connections.
We're planning a winter wedding—ice sculptures, purple dresses,
a *Hello* spread.

I give it six months. When duty's over and done
I'll settle for smashed plates, slammed doors, his tabloid 'tell all',
the quicky divorce.

Then, I'll perch at my tower window,
straining for signs of a warty woman with a wheel and a train of thread.
I'll let my heart zip as she limps through the gates, beckon her in,
hold out my thumb, soothed by the sting of the pin,
The room spinning comfortably again
sleep, sleep warmer, sleep deeper than if I were dead.

# The Wild Life of Goodbye
## Claire Crowther


I worked out how thikes talked, by touch.
They combed that butter-coloured fur with a long revv up
each strand, measuring distance from the head,
pulling or pushing.

They gave each other permission to touch—
the neck, underbelly—and spoke fast. Linguists
charted their range of sounds; semantics, no.
I learned to hear them say:

*Come back to the hollow.* Heard their names.
I have no idea, being a poet, whether they lived in peace
or in violence like their end.
That older female by the traffic island,

hair flattened—how the rush hour traffic rubbernecked
to see her, a thike out of her moat. That mass
of blackening yellow on the *News.*
The cullers left the feet alone.

Thike feet stick to any surface,
their soles a suction-pad beneath boneless muscle.
When someone comes to clear the carcasses,
they'll find a light glue, a smell of fresh

grouting. Its cling could rip your arm off.
Everyone is feral, a deer counts notes, a dog tugs
a child's paw with hands like teeth.
In Hob's Moat today,

an ill pale yolk of sun. Pheasants dashed
into the wood. The male watched the female dip
her head in steaming clay. It was hot
but I didn't notice how short of breath

the sky, how a summer lung can't speak
without breaking. From my eyrie
alongside the *Medieval Fayre*, no homogeny to hair,
hair holds no hegemony for crowns.

*Secrets of the Moat.*
The grass! It's lost its tread. Thunder cruising
makes breeze panic. Against the window, my arms
are strips of silver, run moon solder.

# Sleep, Beauty
Barbara Dordi

Before the spell, you wound inland,
carried barges to the wooden jetty
and waiting gangers glad of work.
They loaded bricks, hay, cement—
horse drawn carts wheeled through your mud.

Ambling ways kept you safe
from wind's heavy knife sculpting
pointed waves, in cahoots with
the scouring tide of the Swale without:
your isolation preserved you.

Spell cast, you left no documents
to furnish sea-dog tales; just
the jetty, ghostly silhouette now,
creek silt-sinking under Progress,
and five decades before the kiss.

# Recruiting Rapunzel
Gillian Laker


Once the tower was home and the witch was mother
and at night she brushed
her daughter's hair

A hundred stokes to make it gleam
a hundred more to make it shine
until it became so fair and fine
and smooth as a rope of silk

The mother held fast to a shrinking core
of appetite and secret spice
ringed like a tree-trunk keeping score
of lean times and plenty

Her daughter's head was always filled
with orange blossom and bridal white
she danced alone to tambourines
and waved to passing strangers

Until the wind changed — the blossoms fell
and the witch's hair turned bridal white
and the strangers began to return her smiles
and howl to gain admittance

And it might have been this
or it might have been that
or the turning years' rat-a-tat
for it wasn't her hair that fashioned the rope
and it wasn't her shape that hung like fruit
or even her knife that cut it down

At least that's what they told her
When they scaled her defences, sprang the locks
and found her brushing a hundred strokes

Now tambourines shake to a different tune
They call out the dead in empty rooms
in draughty halls and shopping malls
in station and airport terminals

And she only remembers
the tower and the rope and the witch
on rainy days of flight delays
as she hands out their words
and smiles and waves
to all the passing strangers

# Soliloquy
Ed Taylor

There was Shakespeare in the park by the lake, and a
picnic and the friend's out-of-town sister, with cancer and
her young daughters, and bread and wine, sweet stuff
being eaten, and the bright clear evening cooled as it
deepened, wind in the mikes and costumes luffing like
sails, and in July the sweaters and jackets came out, the
hoods and hats, and the girls flopped and piled, squealed
and dozed on each other, and not moving or warming was
the pale, slow sister who ate nothing and said nothing, sat
breathing in the chill, until the moon broke over the dark
water and 'All's Well' ended.

# Grandma Cries Wolf

Claudia Van Gerven


Listen!  Is that another knock
on my door? I've slammed the bolt,
drawn the curtains, but still
they find me out. This endless pack
of little girls with their baskets full of poison.

They come shivering, their capes in tatters,
and those cold, slight hands, unpacking their
terrible wicker hampers.

They want me to taste slivers of
their tiny broken hearts pickled
in sour-sweet syrups. They offer me
their ground innards on delicate biscuits.

They want to sleep in my bed, stare
into my sleepless eyes. They want to know everything
about my balding head,

my nose, my false teeth. They want
to warm their icy, forsaken little chests
against my back, my drooping breasts.

I cannot keep them. Were the woodcutter
to chop the forest down, there would never be enough
fire to warm them. So secretly

I call for the wolf, leave a trail of blood to my door.

Let him swallow them whole. Let him take them in.
Let them live in his hungry bowels
Like stones.

# dunyazad
Viki Holmes


but you, little sister,
i want to make you
a world that makes sense

your upturned face
like a flower,
i would have you always
sitting in sunlight

not this dusk, these tales i spin
for my sad lord are meant
for you, beat of my heart,
heart of my world

you see them first: the dreams
i cannot tell, the hoopoe's call,
the stars that slice this canopy of sky

blood-warm, you feel them
as i feel them: talk in stories,
love in words, these sounds
in your ears make my world
make sense.

*Pulling the thread*

# After the Flood
Anne Caldwell


Do you remember the stench of animal hides,
that unholy cramming together,
the racket of snorts,
groans from the lower decks?

Do you recall the creak of the clinker boat,
night after godforsaken night,
the wind in your heart, my sickness,
stalactiting our dreams?

That morning, my darling,
clouds were scuttled. You blinked
into the sun's disc, stared at uncharted water,
fresh archipelagos on the horizon.

Forty days and nights
had turned your lips papyrus-dry.
Our prow nudged land.
Our bodies were two new coins, minted in light.

# It Didn't Happen That Way

Elizabeth Austen

It wasn't a lure, dangled
by some fallen angel.
She found it, mid-path
no tree nearby. Unbruised
red-yellow round

sprung from the gravel.
She entered the sweet
fruit, wet flesh
breaking on her tongue. She didn't
ask for it. Wasn't
looking for it. No one

tempted her. Unless
the apple itself, longing
to be known, can be blamed
for the light bent
across its skin
for the mid-day heat
transforming sugar to scent.

And him? She didn't say
a word to him. He found
her, slack-jawed
skin flushed and damp
as if he had lain on her
pressed into her —

he found her, swallow by swallow
savouring the taste of knowledge
her eyes fixed, focused

somewhere beyond him
as if he no longer existed.
And one more thing—
she didn't tempt him. In fact
she never offered it.

He pried the fruit
from her hand, desperate
to follow, and bit.

## Death of a Taxi Driver

Theresa Heine

It nosed in quietly,
one of those May mornings
that holds its breath,
the city spring idling gently
on the quiet street,
lilac, slick with possibility,
blossom awaiting its cue.

But all we heard,
after the siren
and the urgent feet on the stairs,
were the paws of the cat
padding across the room,
and her yawn, her soft
expelling of air.

# Glasgow Kiss
## Lee-Anne Semple

Aye she's
fair pleased
she got ersel
a lumber
bit
if er maw
cud see
she'd hae
a face
lik thunder.

If er
maw cud
see er
wee gurl
winchin
a hun!
see um
slippin
the tongue!
If er
maw cud
see yon boay
geein er
wee lassie
Buckie an
tryin tae
git lucky.

She wud
pray tae
saint Jude
and finger
er beads
fur god
tae strike
deid the
heathen wi
the ginger
heid.


## Little Red Riding Hood
Angela Gardner


Oh she is the smallest, the prettiest
make ups and dress ups and
*how do I look mummy?* I want to eat

her, little red dress should know better
delicious, how dangerous to stop and talk
I know a house where we can meet

and play a game   the soft inside velvet of her
: I will go this way and you will go that
let's see who gets there first

how large a voice to soften and coax
what strong arms, what legs, what terrible eyes
I have to hold you with

*Tell me, child, what have you brought for me?*

43

# Gretel Takes Control

Rachel Bentham


Candystuffed, we crunch through barleysugar
windows, glassy tongued. We can't get out.

Our teeth shave the chocolate door,
mossy mouthed, jittering for a lemon twist.

Hansel witters for daddy; sugar crazed,
his plump limbs proving like loaves.

The witch plays at gingerbread men, piping
icing buttons down our bellies, big clown grins

foul our cheeks. She licks her fingers, licks
her tombstone tooth as she tucks us in.

I wipe my hands on the bedclothes.
Into the night, I wipe and wipe.

Hansel snuffles; bonbon bottom warm
beside me, under sticky blankets.

At first light she pinches our arms, crooning
*my little sweetmeats* ...sugar tong crone.

She shuts Hansel in the chicken house,
bids me fetch logs for the oven, stoking it high.

A toad squats among the logs, golden eyed.
I bend and kiss him but no prince. He just blinks.

Now! I think as I stride — save him now! Me? Me.
Woodpile oven woodpile oven woodpile oven...

Hansel weeps peardrops, calling to me, his
chubby, grubby hands tight on the chickenwire.

Is it hot enough? Is it hot enough? The
witch peanut crackles in her hopping glee -

Why, put your head in and see, witch: pitch!
Shove! A gammon hiss as her lips kiss coals.

Quick as salt, I snatch the latch
shut. Black sugar eyes pop.

## The Story of a Girl Who Went Forth
Sylvia Fairclough

*after The Story of a Youth Who Went Forth to Learn What Fear Was —*
*Grimms' Household Tales*

Sometimes, my mother shudders when she looks at me.
My sister shudders when she looks at granny. Granny
dribbles and the drips and drops of saliva travel the
channels of her wrinkles. At school the boys snigger at the
hairs curling from the legs of our swimming costumes. The
girls shudder and pull at the elastic cutting into their
thighs. I am a good swimmer. In water I have no inside
and outside; I move easily. No-one knows this except, of
course, the fish. They swim through my body, nuzzling at
soft flesh.

# Camellia Assamica

Stephen Delbos


I met her at the Good Tea Room,
new town's oasis, tucked
down an alley off Vaclav Square.

In one corner, she sat shoeless,
jasmine perfume-scented,
reading Rumi.

Taking tea became our ritual.

Every Sunday afternoon, I poured
my eyes on her across the room,
pretending to read the menu:

Pu-Ehr, Tiger Spring,
    Rolling Clouds,
        Oolong —

Her favorite. Earthy brown,
a taste of smoke that clicked
her tongue.

I preferred a gentle green.

I never understood
the foreign words she used when ordering,
except *Oolong*
blowing like a kiss between her lips.

What conversations
we might have had over tiny cups!
I'd compare tea to poetry:
Both court the tongue and taste
relies on subtlety.

Each night alone, I'd dream the way
we'd steep ourselves between the sheets,
brewing jasmine petals, honey, salt
and sipping till the sun comes up.

I haven't seen her in a month.
But I feel her breath
rise from the kettle
as I check her empty corner again,
cradling, in vacant hands,
a burning cup of Oolong tea.

## Historic Frolic
Meryl Evans

Rumble windy tube, circle pods of Eye,
whoosh up Festival Hall to balcony—
spy Savoy skyline, the Thames sliding by
through onion dog air, past pink floss candy.
Walk Westminster span, dodge traffic jam square
to Crown's brown bark, lakeside shade of willow.
Cross white stucco mall, pass ICA pair,
north to frisky circus, Eros with bow.
Hang a right (black cab speak), there's The Empire,
cheap ticket booth, Charlie Chaplin statue,
tourist clubs and bars—all is here for hire:
Hippodrome, Radisson, lap-dance venue.
Swiss glockenspiel strikes and busker strums licks,
monochrome nuns run to sing-a-long flicks.

# Kilkenny
Fred Johnston

*for Rhona and Siobhán*

I drove out of Kilkenny
Under the whittle moon
Over a bridge mad with laughing

Everyone was made foolish
A cheek-kiss moist as apples
Fallen in a blink from a young tree

A girl as supple as a reed
A woman autumn-haired and sure
Music and music-talk and red wine

I drove out of Kilkenny
Through a scrawl of roads, villages
Black and quiet, turning in dream

The autumn-haired woman
Kissed me for singing, the other
For a poem, and left me sleepless.

# Betty Volunteers a Report on the Paranormal to the Village Board Meeting
John Lehman

First there was this orb, burning right there in
my rearview mirror as I was driving home
from the Piggly Wiggly. Sort of a whitish
yellow that turned orange then red. Just
two nights later, I heard elephant screams. I
will admit those may have been Denny
snoring, but then the following afternoon
my grandson, Todd, told me that when I was
napping I made sounds like elves laughing.
Plus I had a toothache that wouldn't go away.
Next day it was gone. And don't even get me
started on the pot roast that disappeared.

# Unwrapping a Toad
Sue Wood

Start with its skin and feel the rough pucker
that is skin of corpse.
Peel away this to the pith.
The neat plush that rounds its corners
will remind you of over-ripe bananas.
Scoop it away and feel for the bone.
You will see ivory as slight as a bird's thigh.
This is a casket. Pull it open
to where the toad throbs in cold heat.

Consider before you
start to unwrap your toad
that the jewel in its head
is almost certainly alarmed.

# Seal Wife

Heather Harrison

Dry
I finger the coarse white linen
smelling of a blown sun
of seeded lavender, where,
in their quilted wooden cot
these, my white-legged young
curl together, wisps of hair
entwined;
lips that flutter
with echoes of the day's words;
lips that suckle me.

Dry.
They grip with hot, smooth fingers
my tidal heart. But when they cry
why, like the storm's scream,
like the wind that scores a fur head
with flaked ice, like the herring gulls
whose tearing beaks seize my mouth's morsel,
like the Silkie-sisters keening,
then—I am rent.

Their cries wrench the maypole strings
of steel that haul me body from skin.
Should I to the sea-soothe
or cleave to these? Torn from my deep
to Deep?
Toe hearth or wave? Stay? Go?

I wish for water over a lithe tail,
to leave the slicing steps of
my fist-feet on such a scorched land
to play among cool currents
where the moon hatches pearls.

But then must I sever
such sweet cords, such smiles.

I cannot go. Not stay.

The Silkie-Skin he locked away
shrivels and my heart splits, spills salt
daily.


# Pulling the Thread
Ben Parker


He used to say that with enough attempts
the true consequences of any act
would be revealed, like wallpaper, peeled
discloses the room's unseen history.
And so, at parties, in bus queues, on trains
he would seize loose threads on jumpers and pull
and, as far as I know, the thread would break
each time and he'd get shouted at or punched.
But once, I was told, the cotton connected
with a memory of spider's webs
and remained intact while the jumper, loosed
from its moorings, unfurled onto the floor.
He remained calm and continued to tug,
teasing out the cord like you'd coax the truth
from a child. And then the trick,
the silent switch from classic
Newtonian physics to a quantum playground
as cord catches on tendon, tendon on nerve
and with the quick release of a pulled root
sinew un-spooled and flesh and bone
was spun into perfect, fibrous yarn.
Dust motes abandoned Brownian motion,
protons twisted free from the atom's drag
and, if he hadn't quit the scene and fled
the whole Möbius strip of existence
would have unfurled and fallen into line.

# Eurydice: Message from Underground
Marilyn Jenkins


Hades provides amusements: Ixion at his wheel
all day; Sisyphus rock-pushing; Tantalus never
able to satisfy his raging thirst. Even here you're
in clover if Hades and his wife pick  you for
a chum.  Always keep in thick with gods, I say.
I think Hades kidnapping Persephone was so romantic.

Lucky for me, lovely Persephone is not the jealous
type.  We share our stories, everything.  We play
games; make fun of those off the wall loonies the Furies;
drink jugs of crystal water in Tantalus's face. We don't
leave the others in peace, either. Oh how we laugh.
In the end, I didn't miss you at all until my friend

went up top to spend six months with her mother
Demeter.  I was taking note of that keen glance old Hades
gave me, when out of the blue—you turn up, music,
blaring; everything stops. The whole trouble with our
marriage was that bloody lyre. I felt like a widow.
If you'd been around to deal with that snake, I wouldn't

have landed up here at all.  But you were transfixing
tigers, making pine trees do the polka. You could
have sorted a snake, the man who saved the Argonauts
from the Sirens. My father always said I should
have married a man with his feet on the ground,
his eye on the ball who knew his lute from his elbow,

his wife from a lyre. I've been really mad at you
Orpheus. Just one thing you had to remember—DO NOT
LOOK BACK. And what did you do? True to form just
as I was getting somewhere YOU LOOKED.  You know
what they say—when the cat's away ...But watch what kind
of women you go with.  They may not like your music,

not everyone does. They could turn nasty and rip you
to pieces. As for me, don't have a fit—it's just an idea
to save us all grief: Hades is ripe for  my gracious suggestion
If he bites, you can bet - for me there'll be no looking back.
Save yourself a pointless journey; stay up top and stick
to your music. Down here we three make good company.

## Sleeping Beauty
Angela Gardner

They invited the media (denied of course)
*Everyone* came—conspicuous gifts conspicuous perfection
An old woman beside this stretched beauty delivers
a parting gift

*Fifteen years of insatiable wants*
*Nothing that money or fame cannot buy*

And at fifteen court appearances, rehab, private clinics
her parents busy with holidays and careers
Time the skin of an hour. Doctors reassuring them

*She will be saved*
*When she wakes she will not be alone*

the little bitch, small as a handbag, the drug suppliers,
product placers, personal trainers Her on life support
Parents: *no comment*

To wait some time to have a Rich Husband
may be reasonable
but to wait a hundred years while sleeping
is a little strange

(really more than a little strange)

# Jettison
Phil Emery


He lies
spread-eagled
bones awkward
like crepitus stretched out on a broken hourglass plain

a wireless
beached lopsided
longwave chic
crackles out weak weak muzak and desert island downloads

She saunters
rayban insouciance
bathes down
and chin on hands fingers the dial, sways on the bakelite line

from Luxembourg to
Hilversum to Alpha Centauri
the light year programme
While gulls circle and scavenge static she takes a fist of shore

lets it lazily strain
*is this sand this colour or*
*is it me?* he says
*it's you,* she says, and doodles cloud patterns with a fingernail

*And so,* he says, *And so,* she says,
while the tranny crackles a quasar backbeat,
*What's a nice boy like you...*
and strokes the feathery splay of sand and ash and wax

fraying from the blades of his shoulders
Misshapen spittle chariots from his cough
and she daubs 'pig' in another language
through the bright red speckles in the dark stained sand

*Come here often?* he murmurs,
a last cheesy haemorrhaged chat-up line
She rolls onto her back, stretches,
luxuriates against the UV, a fingertip still teasing the tranny...

*That is so antique,* she giggles
*So crucify me,* he comes back, each word alone
She unwinds softly into the air, silent,
thinking about it. Then turns away. *Don't,* he says

She stops. *Leave?*
*Don't.    I have to.*
And she does,
sliding through boundless heathaze,  swaying between melanomas

The sky is botoxed with azure
Not so much as a slash of cirrus
He watches her melt away
Wafting out of the wireless is a play about a woman with a parasol

# Being One of Those
Dylan Jones

Being one of those muggy days
and overwrought
we swam in the thick air
breast-stroke
easily into purple cloud
high above the downs—
what threatened to pull us low
we frittered among the birds:
you opened your throat to sing
and your notes
embodied the weightlessness
we felt
forming a muslin transparency
around us
but flickering with stars—
and suddenly
in a great whorl
separating from the circles
that whirled around us
(blue and white intermixed)
we were carried
higher and higher—
*whoa whoa* we cried
in unison, loudly together
knowing now that there was
no going back
and that we might travel
like two besotted Catherine wheels
upwards and away
revolving around ourselves
moment after moment
staring hopelessly at the earth
disappearing beneath us—
and clinging always
to the last hope of forever.

# briar rose
Viki Holmes


hush! she is dreaming music
sailing on a boat of silk
to the wail of a thousand
saucer-eyed hounds, the gentle
rattle of breaths knocking
together under the blue
china-cup sky

sip! a hummingbird
at her flower-lips,
he makes his way through
the shorn thickets of her hair:
a strand of purplish-red catches
like fire in the flint of his eyes and
a laugh like smoke falls
from her drowsing mouth

we could sleep like this for years
the slow erosion of each day's glib close
forgotten in the hum of dozing thoughts:
the taste of apples lodged at our throat's backs
our bed a case of glass to keep the world at bay

but i would taste your kisses with my open eyes
and mouth, these dreams i trade for the cold air
of morning. wake me, love, i will not fade like those
quaint memories of you and i elsewhere:

the meat turns on its spit,
the maid plucks her black fowl,
i have you with me
and the day lives on.

# The Little Mermaid
## Gillian Laker

She always had
the most magnificent breasts
and hair and arms
and a mouth full of the sea

Not the most conventional of couplings
—perhaps
but in the nip and tuck of the night
as happy as most

He wonders why she has gone
to so much land-locked
lumbering trouble
to split the definitive

He misses the flash
of her salty scales
and the delicate
frill of fin

Diving for pearls
he runs a rasping nettle tongue
between the toes that went to market
and those that stayed at home
sheath wet
and pale as tallow

# Flaming Sue
## Claudia Van Gerven

*after 'Self-Immolation' by Cathy Dwigans in the quilt 'The Sun Sets on Sunbonnet Sue' by the Seamsters Local 500 in Lawrence, Kansas.*

The pinafore was the first to go, gingham bell
that had shaped her obscurity — it never burst
into flame, merely collapsed
in a rain of ash.  As the last remnant of undershirt
drifted lazily above the frenzy of flame,
she realized she had never lived in her flesh
but always in the infantile dress tangled in the thread
of her mother's stitchery.  She had never
searched with child's fierceness the territory
beneath the confines of petticoat, never probed
the body's keen alphabet.

She had been afraid in the beginning — the cold
mechanical stink of kerosene,
the stiff formality of matches —
but in first blue shiver of flame she felt the galaxy peal,
a radiant whisper that spoke all her losses, ferocious
tongues of flame licked her all over, spoke her name
more accurate, more ardent than any lover
she could imagine.

Pain proclaimed the exactitude of nerves,
expressed acutely
the repetitions of her innards.  She knew at last
each winged bone of her spine, glowing, articulate.
Her calves, her belly, the nape of her neck
spoke in tongues ambiguous and precise.
Her toes, her finger ends quavered with mouths
that could never be stitched shut.

*Spindled*

# Skeletons
Kathy Miles

*Newport, 2006*

Boat-buried, his skull smashed
under the hull of a medieval ship.
His ribs entwined with hers,
seawashed, a riddle of bones and wood.
Robust, muscular, he once held his woman
tight, carried fire home in his arms,
fetched food and kindling.

Skeletons under the landscape
move in the swell of waves.
A cradle of sand rocks clavicle or femur,
a pelvic girdle turning to coral.
In my hands might be shells,
or the crushed shards of his spine.
A polished disk, slipped inside the mouth
of a man who died defending his fort,
or harvesting the wheat.

A shine in the slid-back tide
shows white against the water.
He was slurried here in the salt rush
of the estuary, riding the bore
at a full moon, under a hundred bridges
from the marsh, sliding beneath the sterns
of many ships, until he rested
among the chips of bowl and cannon shot.

And here now are the confident seamen
their bold hands full of boat,
easing the sheets, fixing halyard or genoa,
shackles gleaming grease.
Going home to a hot shower,
to a roundhouse of brick and steel.
But above on the hill they are still his sheep,
last of their line: grazing fat and lazy,
good Welsh mutton.

# Frances Bevans
Emily Hinshelwood

*Frances Bevans was buried in St Bride's Haven, Pembrokeshire in 1837
— aged 16*


Some say you were threading a daisy chain
when the edge toppled under you.
At its wildest streak it can do that
— unscripted of course.

Now your stone grave is uplifted by the tide
and who knows, you could be dancing the bay.
Always on the brink of adulthood
forever becoming.

The fisherman has only you in mind,
as he picks his way into the chopsing waves.
The thrash of sea on rock makes friction;
fish dance in strobe light.

He's always at the clash of edges, the fringes,
the moment when the mind unhinges. There
he catches pearls, looks once to heaven and threads them
on a chain — like daisies.


# Kitchen Business
Vahni Capildeo


As if as normal
a bird hit the window
at some speed    just like nothing
it was sitting on the fence
by the time I could realize
that wood and blinking pain
perched outside my head.

# Testing Her Metal

Nicky Mesch

But he could be gentle —
the night he turned her
an inch at a time, painstakingly
slotting the panels of her skirt,
the muscled serpent on his arm
lapping salt as he tightened
the unfamiliar studs at her waist,
oiled her shiny new joints,
buffed the cones
on her breastplate
to a blush.

She shuddered at the glint
spilling from his calloused hands —
waist-length wiry coils,
curly copper lashes,
perfect O for a mouth —
and tried to catch her breath
but already he was easing
metal around her head
and welding it in place.

# The Arachnophobe
Jane McLaughlin

*Little Miss Muffet*
*Sat on a tuffet*

The Equal Opportunities Adviser
said she ought to stop
calling herself Miss
as it was archaic and demeaning
and what sort of a name
was Muffet for a woman
who wanted to break through
the glass ceiling?
Something like Pandora
of Hilary would be
a much better boost
to her career.

The Health and Safety Representative
said that a tuffet
(a three-legged stool)
did not conform
to the safety regulations
and she must replace it
immediately with a properly designed
ergonomic chair
with adjustable seat
and choice of  back positions.

*Eating her curds and whey*

The Environmental Health Officer
took them away for analysis
and prosecuted the farmer
for selling products
made of unpasteurised milk
and went on the six o'clock news
with a warning about an outbreak
of TB in the vicinity.

He also referred her
to the community dietician
who gave her advice
about reducing fat content
and eating five portions
of fruit and vegetables a day.

*There came a big spider*
*Who sat down beside her*

And said: I am the Pest Control Officer
and just in case you are harbouring
any insects, rodents or parasites
I must ask you to complete
this questionnaire.

*And frightened Miss Muffet away.*

Fortunately she had just bought
a new pair of trainers
and was in the next parish in no time.


# Host
Rebecca Goss


Ice cubes bob in the punch like ship wrecked luggage,
a salmon lies pink and sacrificial on its cucumber bed.
Candles line the route of arrival, we welcome

old friends into our home. You move amongst women,
leave your hand on their spines and thoughts in my head.
Stranded with the canapés, I bump between couples,

let the tray tilt long enough to allow one blini each.
Retreating to the kitchen, a fox bolts the garden,
flooding the lawn and my husband with security light.

His new friend leans against the bark of our oldest oak,
her small, dark nipple clasped in his hot, furtive mouth.

# Ice, An Elegy

Helen Moore

The Ice Queen is leaving—
all around, her ancient kingdom
is cracking up—trickling, splitting,
as her vast, crystal sleigh
grinds on the fast-track to oblivion.

For millennia she held her huge mirror
steady to the Sun; now she's losing her cool,
sheets shrinking, her albedo body
pocked with melting pools, moulins
milling in, chutes of water sailing her
the slipway of lost forever.

Yet each day her belly calves
desperate bergs of ice. Bereft, these tongues
curl and shrink as they sense their mother
spent—her skin once tinted blue,
now deathly pale.

Her courtiers and creatures
are disappearing too—
in despair they throw their arms into the air;
tall maidens
once yoked in lustrous bridal gowns,
stagger
one by one
to their knees,
faces crashing down
in mounds into the sea.

Even the glacial snow men,
who plucked boulders and carried
their erratic cargo across continents,
now stumble, retreat—valleys scoured
by their dark rheumatic wake.

Everywhere Foxes, Bears,
Wolverines and Leopards mourn their Queen—
prowling the rosaries of paternoster lakes,
they murmur eulogies and prayers.

And at last we hurry in
with tools, instruments and measuring rods
to probe, extend our senses—
to scientize this demise of ice.


## Selling the Clouds
Ben Parker


One morning we woke to a sky vacant
from the horizon's edge to the very crest
of the taut blue canvas. Not one cloud
mellowed a sky made Mediterranean.
Walking to town, basking in unforecast heat
we turned a corner to see the market
cocooned in a dense grey fog, piled up
and boiling like a candyfloss machine
gone berserk. And in the midst an old man
dressed in souwester and waterproof coat
marionetted among thick damp ropes.
Just to his left, hastily drawn, a sign
listed his prices: he was selling the clouds.
Tethered like giant balloons they buffet
and crash. But as someone walks away
rope in hand, a shape forms then separates.
Cumulonimbus for the new couple,
a taste for the overly dramatic
and the desire to make love in a storm.

# Electrified Sue

Claudia van Gerven

*After the block 'Struck by Lightening' by Carol Gilham in the quilt 'The Sun Sets on Sunbonnet Sue' by Seamsters Local 500 in Lawrence, Kansas.*

She had turned her back
on the cloud, she was walking away
out into undefined space that the cloud made
limitless with its implication of sky.

And the movement itself was better still,
the sense of direction. If there is cloud,
there must be sky, if there is sky there must be
latitude, scope for her fettered vision
all the peripheries beyond the tunnel of the brim.
She could survey more than the plod of her feet,
be subject to distractions of frontiers.

When the bolt hit her, the jolt
shook the alignment of stiff vertebrae.
Suddenly her feet leapt from the ground,
kicked up higher than a Rockette, her head snapped
back to a glimpse of unbonneted  sky.
She became aware of a certain double
jointedness, the ease with which she might
slip into postures other than her wonted
uprightness, feet orienteering
unmapped terrain.

# Stoned Again
Paula Balfe


We're rocking hard and wild on Friday night,
On boulders breaker-beaten, smooth and cool.
Wailing, beaching, bladdered in the moonlight,
Screeching out the same old chorus. And who'll
Be first to chuck, I wonder — when this chav
Comes over, Nike trainers shifting foam
And shingle, flashing steel. Scary? Should have
Stayed at home, sweetie. Should have stayed at home.
*Hey you, Medusa! Wanna give some head?*
He gargles through his lager. I don't think
So. And the rutted myth comes good, stones dead
His mortal gaze. Amazing! Not a blink.
Look here, guys — it's great to be an eyesore.
Don't I have the perfect face to die for?


# Nihil Sine Laboure
Lee-Anne Semple


A pubescent hooded cluster
Appeal for rizla and ginger
From the pastel ice-cream van

Chip wrapper tumbleweeds
Float down the street
Like dirty wedding confetti

A billion tiny cubes of glass
Make a puddle on the path
Like risky crystal dice

A crinkly sheet of corrugated iron
Warns *Watch Yourself*

# broken wing rook
Steve Ely

*found dead under hawthorns on saturday twelfth may two thousand
and seven after surviving grounded since mid-march*

there it goes again the broken wing rook hop flutter
waddling away dragging its crippled wing across the just
sown barley field the rest of the feeding rookery flapped
off beyond the hedge horizon what does it feel when
theyre all gone and its left alone to face its death three
weeks now since the lead shot that left the other dead on
the bridlepath smashed its primaries secondaries tertials
and left it a hobbled pedestrian hop flutter waddling away
through barbed wire fences tangling through brambles
and bristling hawthorns three grounded weeks in this
ordinary place where stoats drag screaming leverets and
buzzards circle crying like cats and the big female
sparrowhawk knocks ring doves from the sky and each
morning brings cleaned mallard breastbones feathered
wings attached that lad with the pellet gun that bloke with
the lurchers those kids on mountain bikes bill cooper with
his twelve bore three weeks maybe it can make it to the
moult after all if it's just feathers and not the wing itself
maybe it can make it all through the summer facing a
dozen different deaths a dozen times each day there it
goes again hop flutter waddling away three weeks already
it just might make it i hope it can

# Caribou Infant

Dylan Jones


So the little calf
the caribou infant
sits patient beside

the red, rubbly heap
of its once-mother
whose strong, resourceful

body has become
a two-day banquet
for the wolves & bears

the little one is patient
something in the dead heap
still speaks of *mother*

 a scent of the cold, fixed
carcass still promises
milk & confidence:

for two days of sun & moonlight
in the friendly grasses
the little calf waits

for resumption of accustomed ways—
for life (that will soon be over)
to up and re-begin—

for the journey (that is ended)
and the easy pickings (never to be had)
and the long, slow wanderings


(even trembling cannot last forever)

# The Gloucestershire Argonauts
## Elizabeth Speller

That winter we ran aground.  Water
stretched as far as Lechlade spire, sucked
thick round squat willows, silenced the lock gates,
where the old bridge still rigged, heaved on its pilings
and roads lay low beneath the flood
and somewhere in the moving plain between
the stones and the earth the abandoned river
scoured and tugged.

Unstoppable.

We laid fortifications: sacks of sand along each small,
forgotten breach where the water might
make an entrance.
Caulked house and thoughts against the mud
and the mess and the dark.
But the river lapped and coiled and called in the night
and our breath betrayed us, running wet
down the glass.

Hazed with burning oil, the house ached
damp to its bones;
Dogs pee'd on the floor, the baby coughed,
and the water rose—
moulds clustering in the flutes of curtains, spore-bursts
smudged across a wall;
rose and kept us at bay, small before our fire,
reeking of paraffin;
rose from underneath, milky with lime
and the smell  of old river,
beading the stone skin,  slippery  with sweat.

No sailor attempting the measure of a flat world
was smaller than my father, toiling our slight boat
in absent fields
letting the current find his him,
trusting that some watery fortune would see him sound.

# Head of the Family
Theresa Heine


Colours nailed to the mast
she breasts the swell
of a riotous sea.
Settlers' blood pounds like rum
through her veins, landmasses
heave into her horizons,
as Mrs Noah yodels the name
of every mermaid, thrusts an ear
against every shell.

Bustling below deck
she battens down the butterflies,
re-coils the snakes
and pacifies the doves.

Her children toss in her wake,
craning after rainbows,
thin fingers clutching at marker buoys,
hair strung out on the wind.

But her husband,
bobbing along behind
in his battered lifebelt,
dreams of lying in the garden,
stroking the curve of a wrist
as if it were a flower.

# Beating the Dormant Season
Barbara Dordi

*In February, 2001, 24 year old Ellen MacArthur finished second in the
25,000 mile Vendée Globe Circumnavigation, in her boat 'Kingfisher'.*


Winter's sodden earth
dried by fierce easterlies
is suddenly lighter

                    Westerlies drive this
                    challenger from Derbyshire
                    but which course to choose

fine combed land
virgin brown in readiness,
the spinning earth still

                    surfing Brylcreme-smooth
                    or tacking tousled seas
                    beneath black-and-blue skies

snug inside their glass
palaces, smug seedlings cheat
the dormant season

                    Kingfisher cocoons
                    technological know-how
                    and the catnap kid

expectant drills filled,
roots firmly anchored in,
sap slowly rising

                    spinnaker furled,
                    stitching, reefing,
                    monster mainsail mended

angry skies calm,
cold as silence, frost snakes in
searching for weaklings

                    clawing to windward
                    dagger-boards crack
                    canvas snaps

after winter wiles
none but the fittest
sail into spring

                    beating into les Sables d'Olonne
                    to cries of
                    *Vivre, Jeanne d'Arc!*

the sapling from land-locked
Derbyshire wins everything
but the race.

## Annunciation
Sally Douglas

I've always been a reasonable man—
now reason's rasped like sawdust to the ground.
I've measured angles: sawn, and planed,
and nailed; created useful things. But now,
you twist and flicker like a flame
licking dry tinder, aching to consume.

The way things dovetail—joints and bonds—
the making of a serviceable thing:
that's all I know.
Not signs and sins and angels. Not
shining veils that darken with strange light.
I'm just a craftsman. I can't make
solidity from ashes. But nor can I withstand
the heat of you—aroused by God's own hand.

# Spindled
Helen Ogden

Over land my suitors came, bloody
before they hacked at thorns
to get to me, no one
told them I was

a lazy child, took to
my bed often, spat out good food
served on golden platters. *Oh Briar Rose,*
the King would say, *our pretty*
*daughter lights up the world!* Drunk.
I wiped wine from my lips. Swaggered like
a lady shouldn't. As much sugar
as I could swallow
hung from a threaded bag
around my wrist.

Until they found me,
sucking smoke from a candle, pulled
me by the hair over gilded tiles. Ditch
Witch. Anything wrong, rotten, at risk, sharp
taken from me. So unfair,
even my corset lacings
cut with a long blade.
As if I would.

Asleep, subjects hollowed
out my mouth with their fingers. Rawrubbed
me clean. They cut my hair, gave
my split ends
to the birds. No one
would have me now. They made sure

there are some things you
never wake up from.

# Cinderella
Angela Gardner


She may be beautiful but where was her invitation?
And us two days lost to liposuction & enema practitioners
to shoehorn into the *perfect* red dress

We wanted the bloke with the money to notice us
so we say yes, and yes and of course yes
but 4am the stupid bloke follows the upstart party-girl.

Then he thought he would test it with all the girls
he may not look too hard but even he has standards

*Everything about her says webcam*
*or this is how but cheaper*

Window shopping after all—what a charmer!

Who says *we're* the ugly sisters? Us two sisters
lipidly home to gloat (eventually)—*baby hippo skin*
sheathed in red dresses loud and swaying act a mock wedding

No the bloke with the money won't come at it
magazine makeover princesses don't do it for him

# Meltdown
Bill Trüb


The night sky is a blackboard I near
on a Thursday, but Thursday is Thor's day.
A thunderbolt cracks my forehead, clears
my mind. I become a vegetable. I sputter clichés.
My verbs and subjects doesn't agree.

I orbit.

On Friday night, the moon is hungry.
It eats a smorgasbord of stars, straps a corset
around its white gut. Earthlings snap their necks to gawk
as it spews half-chewed stars. Faster than an astronaut,
I dash to the blackboard with a stick of pink chalk.
I don't know whose skin I'm in as I connect the dots
of Orion, his angular jaw, his love handles. I melt
down to my knees in front of him. I unbuckle his belt.

# The Green Pea Falls in Love
Geoff Lowe


The pea, the pea-green pea, was unconcerned
after being spilled from the pod.
Nor did it worry about losing touch
with its pea-green brethren.

Here, near the hedge side,
it was nice and quiet,
with plenty  of  open   space.
And being precariously perched
on a low-slung nettle leaf
added some piquancy to its existence.
Life on the outside
was throbbingly exciting.

Almost on a roll,
the pea observed non-round things,
and the back legs of a spider
that was on the prowl.
Then it was startled by the suddenness
of a large and all-encompassing flop.
The weight of a banana skin,
hurled by some passer-by,
might easily have crushed the pea,
but for the springy cushioning of the nettle bed.

When things settled down at a gentle angle,
the pea shuffled along to explore
the soft, cosy underside of the floppy banana skin,
now melting a little in warm welcome
and becoming — oh so deliciously slippy.
We needn't go into the raw details
of what happened next,
(and who can say
whether the pea and the banana skin
lived happily ever after).

But, for a while,
they certainly had a lovely time.

*What the weaver knows*

# In this movement of air

Charles P. Ries


We stand in twilight
knowing meaning will
come as it always does.

Some things are beyond our
control:

> The migration of birds
> The end of love
> The Harvest moon
> The inevitability of war

Some things just happen.

This ebb and flow are as
fixed and predictable as the
certainties of gravity.

Raising our eyes toward the night
sky we embrace beneath a rain
of falling leaves, and celebrate
the autumn of our time here.

# What Brings Us Together
Sally Bliumis-Dunn


I dream I am building
with beach glass—

brown, green and white pieces,
an occasional royal blue.

I glue each piece to the edge of another.
What I am building is hollow,
so the light shows through;

it is wider at the base,
and tapers to a point

like a giant upside down icicle.

At first I am building on a tar-stained lot,
then it switches to our yard
in the grass, and I see you

walking toward me, waving something
like a letter.

You don't ask what I'm making.
And because it's a dream,
I don't mind.

We are talking through
the language of things:

the sculpture's beauty is
what brings you to me,

just like the paper you're holding,
makes me

stop what I'm doing
with glass and glue

and move towards
you waving your hand.


## Ciao!
Meryl Evans


The workers are stranded, the locals are lost,
stalking the streets for strong tea and white toast.
The Romans, defeated by burger bars and bistros,
are back home with their Gaggias under Bardi stars.
The new chain has launched another logo-littered coffee house
of designer chrome and leather, through see-me plate glass.

Tall-tales and troubles remain unsaid.
The jukebox has spun the last vinyl hit.
There's no pasty to steam and no chip to egg-dip.
The ketchup's congealed.
The last cuppa's been slurped.

On slick skin we sit, on slick skin we sit.

# Persephone
Maria Wilson

*for Rachel*

The buzz of a lime bug alerts
my senses, once more drawing
hazy eyes from the yellowed paper
into the garden.

How long had I been holding tight
these pages, whilst the black print
softened before me,
then lay unread?

The bug settles on the grass, explodes
into green. Wild cerise roses,
thick and thorny, crawl, then stretch
up to a blue, blue sky.

And you, my brave one,
who left our place and time,
travel, somewhere now,
beyond mud and fog
underworldy.

I dream of rusty struts, sodden wood, a falling
down mansion, a knot of passages, a floor slick with algae.

In the cobalt three seagulls circle.
White doboks, shirts and socks float
in the breeze, which licks
at my arms and the backs of my knees.

A black eye glints, appeals, sucks you back. Darkness.

Clouds of silver and white nudge
past purple geranium, then tumble,
blossom heavy, over
the stones beneath.

Beside me, my lover sleeps,
dozes and sleeps,
brow and cheek flushed
and golden. Hand, heat damp.

Listen

the coo of a wood pigeon,
distant laughter,
the light ring of chimes.

Here      it is summer.

# Crossing the Water
Anne Caldwell


My homeland is a faint smudge of charcoal,
the scrum of Liverpool dock fading from memory.

I watch that warm frill of silt as the River Mersey
empties her sandy skirts into the brine.

Wind tugs the loose canvas of the Irish sea.
The *Aquatania* pitches in the swell like a pot of paint.

Thousands of knuckles have gripped this rail,
watched the watercolour of their country slip from sight.

My stomach churns like a steam turbine,
breath pinched by a thumb and a forefinger of fear.

The edge of my ticket
imprints itself through the silk lining

where you used to
stroke my thighs, stretch my white skin.

I was the palest woman you'd ever seen,
your soft, tapered fingers like sable brushes,

the fingers of a man who'd never laboured,
knew to ask a woman what she likes.

You named me your water sprite,
traced blue streams on my skin's map,

murmured you wouldn't let me out of view
in case I grew a turquoise tail.

I picture the hills where we used to walk,
a brushstroke of clear thought:

our serpentine nature—legs wound together,
making love one early June in Coniston water.

Life was once bright as a sac of eggs.
You had yet to abandon your art,

turn your frustration into barbed wire
spooled across the gateway to your heart.

I rip up your letters as the ship
swings towards Ellis Island.

Behind me, paper darkens.
Ink blooms like algae.

I sense the slowing of the engines
through hardwood, stare

at the Statue of Liberty rising out of the mist,
skyscrapers—a giant art gallery above my head.

# Me Daedalus, You Daughter

Lisa K. Buchanan

I can see from your fiery eyes that you've heard quite
enough about Icarus, and yet, when your latest sort-of-
date-but-more-a-friend-with-benefits is waiting at the door
and you float down the stairs in sub-equator jeans and
hoop earrings with your fuchsia lace bra pushing up out of
your tank top, pushing up what was not there last year and
perhaps not even there this year, offering your heart in the
form of a small, red tattoo, I worry that you're courting an
upward doom; that instead of eliciting his affections, the
aeronautical contraption will compete; that your sort-of
date will want to appeal to your genuine heart but be
seduced by the ivy-twined, glittering one on your cleavage;
that during the movie he will reach for the popcorn and a
deliberately uncalculated sniff of your hair, but collide
with the padded plumage that has usurped even the
territory of snacks; that later when the car radio has gone
mute along with everything the two of you might have
talked about, an accusing silence is spawned by the terror
of boring each other; that when the device is undone and
your inky valentine sinks before his eyes, returning your
topography to one found in nature, you will feel you must
compensate, must distract your friendly beneficiary from
the plunge, must exceed the initial illusion with the greater
beguilement of arts unknown; that your breezy ascent
begets the flame that melts your waxen wings.

# Feeling a walk
Dylan Jones


Feeling a walk
within me, at dark
pre-dawn, when fields
open like history—
entering, I tread
carefully, reading
their movements—And
the dead come alive—
my father, for one,
pushing himself up
a hill, in excess, but
making it—
And old Aunt Emily, like
a Belsen unfortunate, but
victim of her mind's privation;
she sits where the stream
divides, hunched in her
favourite chair; on
her brittle lap
Peter the cat
opens his dark eyes—
And suddenly the hillside
busies itself with shape
after shape—and not
being sheep or stone
I might choose
to companion them—
confronting the sleeping light
together, in the cold
loneliness that is theirs.

# Journey
Bill Trüb


West, inside the belly of a boy, east
echoes in his ears, north is a lift drifting
up his spine, south blinks a blind eye.

Open-faced every Monday morning,
closed-minded by Friday's slow walk
into the weakened weekend, he sleeps

without dreaming in Lisbon International,
awakes barefooted, a tale on his tongue,
fresh bite mark in his passport.

Unbound by borders, he glides over rails
in a second-class carriage, a determined dusk
grows into midnight, clumsily hung over Spain.

But colors soon enter his rearview, orange
burns through a gloom-gray sky, he speaks
Spanish in stutters to a stranger full of truths.

He smells the perfume of a busy fish market,
a woman wraps snapper in *El Pais*, a girl dribbles
a football around a fruit stand.

He traps this scene inside his skull,
later he'll box it into stanzas, gift-wrap it
in rhyme and give it away for free.

But there's a journal in his rucksack
kept only for himself. And there's a cloud
that downpours in his head sometimes

and, sometimes, he fattens the albatross
around his neck with sticks of chocolate
and the journey means more.

# Discovery

Rebecca Goss

*The prettiest woman I ever kissed was another man's wife,*
*my dear mother 1941-2005.*
>            —Tattoo on man's back, Liverpool, summer 2006.


Undiscovered last night, the tattoo
is obvious now. Morning lets me see

what I traced blindly in sweat, affords me
clear view its inky crawl across tight,

tanned skin. Black curling loops at the base
of your back, the spot I made arch

when I locked my ankles there.
And just as unease shudders over me,

a slow turning in my throat, you wake,
roll over, whisper what you want. Lure me

to finger the deep ridge of your spine,
where I will find it, rising, like Braille.

# listen, and i will tell you
Viki Holmes

she is dreaming again:
djinns and sherbert
cave mouths and genii
they are in love with words,
this pair, rain from her mouth
like kisses

on his oiled beard, proud chin:
he will not touch her, though she is
moon-pale, dewy as twilight
but he will grasp at her stories,
coast like a trireme on these
swelling tides: there is
no rest for them,

they have not touched,
these lovers, yet she blushes
at his look, she knows his need
to hear, her need to speak.

the nights go on.

perspiration
beads his brow, her lip
the perfumed air is warm
they have forgotten all but
when the story ends
and where it starts:

infinity plus one, they do not
wish to draw apart, the sun will rise
when, heavy-lidded, they retire.

she dreams of listeners, now:
he is her own reflected voice
she does not live, except at night,
his cushioned gaze on hers.


# Taking the Wheel
F. M. Nicholson


My mother could never drive
across the Great Plains—*Too flat.*
*You can go straight for three days,*
she swore, *I'd fall asleep. Give me*
*mountain roads any time.* So she attacked
the Rockies, the Sierras, gleefully wrenching
the huge wheel of the Rambler station wagon
near ridges, through narrow passes, curling
the blind turns with abandon. My father
was handed the long, grueling stretches:
Iowa, Nebraska. He could stay focused
through anything, driving straight through
to the edges of a 21-year marriage. Then
he fell off.
Mom didn't see that twist coming.
We kids sat quiet in the back seat,
making companions out of pipe cleaners—
our job to sway with the shifting load
as they drove.

# The Politics of Fear

Sylvia Fairclough

The seaside on a summer's day,
a chips and vinegar fingers day.
Ice cream for me
and then a hot and sticky
tea in Evans Street with aunts:
strong sugary brew and bread
as thick as stokers' arms.
Driving home, we pass the docks
where dad once worked,
still tar-grimed black
though coal-less now.

A photo-call...

just him and mum,
embedded in a dockland view.
Wary of the edge, she turns away.
I watch him grab her wrist
and turn her to the void
between the ship and quay.
Stay close, he says,
for if you fall you'll drown
in oily scum; trapped
and crushed by the heaving hull.
Ground like a snail
beneath a man's heel.

They smile for the camera.

# Emma Bovary's Ink
## Mim Darlington

the dip and scratch of it
the bruise of blue
into parched white

each time
the quill held it
with tension so delicate

as if it were the blood she lacked
the scent of hot wax
solid, red as her lips

it patterned loops and curls for her
like the drooping collar of lace
the pearls on her skin

it traced through her veins
drew quivering pictures
from the warm bone of her head

the coils of her hair
round fingers in lamp-light
the smooth hand
the drowning love of the page.

# Gorgeous Fool
Fred Johnston


They said about the village she was beautiful
in the way they'd nod up a Spring day
and that she could have had any lad, but chose
a solid man who couldn't tell a tulip from a rose —

Men envy her like women in the supermarket,
following her with their eyes, confused
that what's stirred in them is heart-born, not
earthy but fleshed in air, yet no less hot.

At thirty she does what her mother dictates
and can't drive, so takes her daughter walking
as far as the Post Office with her eyes on
the ground; at tea-time, her husband comes along.

This village marks her starting out and end
it is the map of her: but once, young mothers
say, she was wild with the rest of them, before
some mad sense of rightness banged the door.

So now she's gorgeous as the sea is,
bright-haired, wheat-bright, reed-supple,
reed-slim, supple as a branch in a gale —
gorgeous as a well-made suit, or a folk tale.

# Interview With Abelard

Ed Taylor

*what's it like*
well you know
when in movies
someone's on
a train crying
& another someone
a lover, runs
along the platform
crying, arms
reaching toward
the 1st someone
as the train teases
both with nearness
then shrugs & gets on
with business—
it's like that
pretty much
forever

# The Fairy-Tale Heroine Leaps from the Page

Pam Thompson

Midnight.

Behind me,
the terrible forest, a trail of stones
sown by orphans,
a yellow brick road ,
a wolf doing a striptease in the garden.
No more, the seven league boots,
the blood-red pumps, the sharp glass slippers.

My feet were bare and white as a baby's dream.
I'd dumped the giant, dissed the prince.
Now I leapt through fields shod only in late rain,
then early dew.

Sun up. Footsore, bleary.
And behind
me, midnight, its last last stroke.

# Red Riding Hood
Seonad Plowman

She walks in with her
six inches, plates pirouetting on every
finger. The suits follow her, she's
liquid on the tiled floor.
A splash of blusher, printed precisely
the morning after.
She swims from table to
table, eavesdropping on every
deal, every secret,
smiling as she cleans up
tomato ketchup stains.
She's forgotten puking up
at 3 a.m. last night.
She leaves with that stranger
on table 19 (black coffee with sweeteners).
Whilst putting on her red coat she
sees the reflection, his teeth, tiny
specks of chalk on the
morning specials board.

# The Invention of Tarka

Mim Darlington

*for Henry Williamson*

No one can say how
he came to the water
how he plucked pebbles
from the river's pockets
and made thoughts—

no one can say how the night
made nostrils, whiskered its way
from the roots of an oak
how its rudder thickened
with the wind, or the storm
muscled a heart out of the  moor—

but one man saw a wanderer in the stream
hid himself in moss and rock
watching night after night
named it Tarka—
*Little water wanderer*

saw it in the paws of the river
as they clawed starlight
yickering at distant wars—
and under its pelt he crawled
followed tracks along Torridge and Taw
two sets of prints in the slicking silt
man and otter, beside the edge
where all the rivers meet
and pour into a wider view.

So who can say when the eel learnt fear
or the trout first felt speed shiver in its sides?
All I can say is, when Tarka swims
all the water leans toward him
frays air into a swilling of pearls
and streams love themselves more deeply —

and at that moment
poetry nosed its way into the world
took its place among the four elements
made them five
and now
when night silks the water
the weave in it says
*hush, keep it secret.*

# O is for Olga
Kristine Ong Muslim

The orderly talks to me using the tone of someone who is
speaking to a four-year old. Sometimes, I think I deserve it.
Humility is a good thing to learn after burning my
daughter's house down when I cannot stand the cold.
At 9 a.m. every morning in my room, I watch the windows
become skulls with the sun in their eyes. They are the
multiple personalities of God.

# Death of a Unicorn

Nicky Mesch

He almost let her touch him once—
too intent on the scent of the ruby-trimmed cloak
dewing on the grass—her fingers
a horn's breadth from his burr-tangled mane
when he snickered and sidestepped away.

Even a desiccated virgin might tire
of waiting, choose instead to smudge ugliness
with smoky candlelight and rough wine.
Perhaps she'll catch a burly sailor's eye
in a quayside tavern, follow him
into a narrow alley, where she'll pretend
his rum-soaked bristles reek of fresh grazed grass
and the shimmer on his coat isn't the rust
of one hundred fishhooks.

Easier to flee, through crooked streets,
over the bridge—past the ruby-crusted castle
her sister married into—stumbling
and crashing, brambles tearing her skirts,
roots tripping her silk slippers,
until she falls headfirst and heaving
into the hollow at the clearing's edge.

Let this be the night he comes to her,
kneels at her feet, places his muzzle
in her lap. Let him breathe hot
and moist on her skin.

If she raises her eyes she'll find
the image full flesh in front of her—
unicorn and ruby-ringed slut rutting
in a blade of moonlight.

The following twilight she'll return
stained with her sister's scent.
Shivering in a blood-trimmed cloak,
she'll cling to shadow
at the edge of the clearing
and wait.

# The Widow
Aleah Sato

I read the letter again. The frozen ship is still locked in ice.
You hold the helm. You sent a gull to tell the story. I could
do two things. I fold the letter, shove it under the couch.
The air in the room chokes me. The walls scorn. I wear
dresses made of curtains. I was born to be a piece of china
or a candlestick. I was sent to react by rolling up with the
carpet. My children have flown to China. They record the
weather and learn lullabies on the pipa. Still I wait. They
are so brave.

You send another letter. You plead. I fold up the letter,
chew on some gum. My bird flits in her cage. I was made
to watch the singing. I close the doors and sweep the halls
with my eyelashes. Another letter is a map I tattoo on my
left breast. Another is a promise of treasure. What use have
I for gold? There's so much to be done here. The stairwell
waits for disarray. My hair is locked in a trunk by the bed.
And there are so many dresses to wear. Ah, my love, if you
could only see this living I do.

# What the Weaver Knows
Wendy Klein


She's not just any maiden lounging in the millefleurs,
there to bait the trap. On her canvas, invisible

to the innocent, fish knives gleam, wait to scale
your silver, crack open your heart. Listen;

there are rumours of drowning by metaphor:
the flicker of dance, the aspiration of flight,

the whale-bone squeeze that robs breath, moulds
flesh into enticement, promises nothing.

Embrace the rush of darkness, the drip and seep
of 4 a.m. when eyelids are peeled back, lashes bat

and flap, when the tick of the body is loudest as light
advances, twists, morphs, begins its birth trial:

crown of head, shoulders, the buttocks' heart-cushion,
legs and feet, their twitch and kick built-in.

No she's not just any maiden there to bait the trap, a silly pawn
in some hunter's game. It's the beast she covets:

the arch of his back, his mane's rough silk, the heave of his
white, white breast. Look out, for only the canniest will

break into the spiked circle, where she spell-spins;
a sucker for unicorns; not much of a lady.

# Contributors:

**Arlene Ang** is the author of *The Desecration of Doves* (iUniverse, 2005), *Secret Love Poems* (Rubicon Press, 2007) and *Bundles of Letters Including A, V and Epsilon* (Texture Press, 2008), co-written with Valerie Fox. She lives in Spinea, Italy. More of her writing may be viewed at www.leafscape.org. Her poetry collection is published by Cinnamon Press in 2010.

**Gail Ashton** is an ex-academic and teacher, now a freelance writer and editor. She is the author of a poetry collection, *Ghost Songs*, and co-editor of *Only Connect*, both by Cinnamon Press, 2007. Her poems and short stories have appeared in numerous magazines and anthologies. She has also published a number of academic books and study guides, including many on medieval poetry.

**Elizabeth Austen** served as the Washington state 'roadshow' poet for 2007, and provides weekly commentary on Pacific Northwest poetry readings on KUOW 94.9, public radio, Seattle. Her audio CD, *skin prayers*, is available at elizabethausten.org.

**Paula Balfe** is a registered nurse and complementary therapist living in Stubbington, Hampshire. She began writing poetry in her teens and was published a few times, but other commitments were more pressing and her Muse took a back seat for several years. Making up for lost time, she graduated from the University of Portsmouth in 2007 with a first class Honours degree in English and Creative Writing. Her poetry has appeared in *Iota, Reach, The Dawn Treader, Obsessed With Pipework* and *Other Poetry*.

**Rachel Bentham**, poet, playwright and aspiring novelist, says: I teach at Bath Spa University. Many of my stories and plays have been broadcast on BBC Radio 4. I am a Royal Literary Fellow at Cardiff University, and spent several happy years living in Swansea as a child, loving the beaches of the Gower. I am currently enjoying writing a rather provoking and rude historical novel.

**Sally Bliumis-Dunn** teaches modern poetry at Manhattanville College and SUNY Purchase. Her first book of poems, *Talking Underwater*, was published by Wind Publications in 2007. In 2002, she was a finalist for the Pablo Neruda Prize. She lives in Armonk, New York with her husband John.

**Lisa K. Buchanan's** fiction and essays have won awards and appeared in numerous magazines. She lives in San Francisco and at www.lisakbuchanan.com

**Anne Caldwell** was born in London and grew up in the North West. She now lives in a Pennine village with her son and works for the Open University and NAWE. Her poetry has previously been published in a range of anthologies— *Poet's Cheshire* (Headland) and *The Nerve* (Virago), *Only Connect* (Cinnamon), *The Ground Beneath Her Feet* (Cinnamon). She is currently featured in *Red Ink 4* and her first pamphlet collection, *Slug Language,* is published by Happenstance Press.

**Vahni Capildeo** (b. Trinidad, 1973) works freelance for *The Oxford English Dictionary* and *The Caribbean Review of Books*. Her poetry includes *No Traveller Returns* (Salt, 2003); *Person Animal Figure* (Landfill, 2005); *The Undraining Sea* (Norwich, Eggbox, forthcoming 2009); *Dark and Unaccustomed Words* (Norwich, Eggbox, 2010). *One Scattered Skeleton* (prose non-fiction: Trinidad, England, Iceland, memory) is excerpted in Iain Sinclair's *London: City of Disappearances* (Penguin, 2006), *The Caribbean Review of Books*, *The Arts Journal* (Guyana), and *Stand*. Work in progress is *Static* (short stories) and *Utter* (poetry).

**Ian Clarke** writes: Born Wisbech, Cambridgeshire and currently working at Leeds Metropolitan University. Published widely in small press magazines and various anthologies. Latest pamphlet, *A Trickle of Friction* (Hub Editions, 2003), available from the author.

**Claire Crowther's** first collection, *Stretch of Closures*, was published in 2007 by Shearsman and was shortlisted for the Jerwood Aldeburgh Best First Collection prize. Her poems and reviews are widely published in such journals as *Poetry Wales*, *New Welsh Review*, the *Times Literary Supplement* and the *London Review of Books*. She has an MPhil in Creative Writing from Glamorgan University and is currently poet in residence at Dorich House, a museum devoted to the life and work of twentieth century sculptor, Dora Gordine.

**Mim Darlington** is an English teacher and lives in Devon where she works as a poet and freelance writer. She performs at open mic events, at festivals in a duo called 'The Honeytongues,' and is a member of Moor Poets, a group of writers from Dartmoor. Her first collection, *Windfall*, is published by Oversteps Books.

**Stephan Delbos** is a New England-born poet living in Prague, where he teaches, edits *The Prague Revue* (www.thepraguerevue.com) and hosts The Prague Poetry Workshop. His work has appeared most recently in *Dirty Napkin*, *Born Magazine*, *Alehouse*, *Rain Taxi* and *Poetry International*.

**Marilyn Donovan** is from Cheshire. A degree at Sheffield University, studying under the great William Empson, was followed by several months working in the Pen-y-Gwryd Hotel, Gwynedd, before moving to the Science Library at the University College of North Wales. She married a member of the Mountain Rescue Team based at RAF Valley and spent ten years on Ynys Môn before they moved to Dover. Some three years ago she took voluntary redundancy from library work to spend more time writing. Since then Marilyn's poetry has appeared in such magazines as *Orbis*, *The Interpreter's House*, *ARTEMISpoetry* and *South*. She is currently working on a novel.

**Barbara Dordi** edits *Equinox*—a poetry journal, and *The French Literary Review*, a twice-yearly journal which publishes poems, short stories and articles with a French connection. (www.poetrymagazines.org.uk) The latest of her six poetry publications, *Entre-Deux*, written in English and translated into French, is a celebration of life in France. In 2009, Cinnamon Press is publishing Barbara's collection *Moving Still*.

**Sally Douglas** lives in Devon, with her husband and three children, and works in education. She has had poems published in a number of magazines, including *Smiths Knoll*, *iota*, *Acumen* and *The Interpreter's House*, and poems and a short story in *The Ground Beneath Her Feet* (Cinnamon Press, 2008). She is currently working on a poetry collection, so the only spare time she has is when she is asleep in bed.

**Steve Ely** writes poems, short stories and is currently editing his novel, *San Benito Brother*. His work, including extracts from his huge poem JerUSAlem, can be found in a range of venues in print and on the web, including www.laurahird.com, www.dogmatika.com, *The Slab of Fun*, *The Savage Kick*, *The Lilies & Cannonballs Review*, *Literary Chaos* and others. 'broken wing rook' is from his collection-in-progress, *the compleat eater*.

**Phil Emery** works as a writer and lecturer and teaches creative writing at Keele University. His work has been published in the UK, USA, Canada and France. The poem 'The Birth of Merlin' was recently published in *Pendragon*, a journal of Arthurian studies—and a short story, *ID* was broadcast on BBC radio in 2007. The play *Sirens*, set in Cornwall, was performed in 2006 at Coventry and Staffordshire Universities. His novel *Necromantra* is published by Immanion Press (http://www.immanion-press.com)

**Meryl Evans** was born in Ynyswen, Rhondda Fawr. She has lived and worked in The Arts in Treorchy, Swansea College of Art and in London as a graphic designer and calligrapher and is now based in Llantwit Major.

**Sylvia Fairclough** was brought up in Longbridge, Birmingham. She now lives and works in Bath, and Gwynfe, Carmarthanshire.

**Angela Gardner** was born and brought up in Wales and now lives in Australia. She is the winner of the 2004 Bauhinia Open Poetry Prize and the 2006 Arts Queensland Thomas Shapcott Prize for Poetry. Her first book *Parts of Speech* was published in 2007 by University of Queensland Press. She was the recipient in 2007 of a Churchill Fellowship enabling her to travel to the USA and UK to investigate small press publications. She is the co-founder with Kerry Kilner of Light-Trap Press which also publishes the online poetry journal *foam:e* (www.foame.org) She is a 2008 recipient of a Visual Arts and Crafts Strategy grant to produce two artist's books and in 2009 will travel to Ireland on an Australia Council Literature Board residency at the Tyrone Guthrie Centre. Angela is a practising visual artist with work in national and international public collections.

**Rosie Garland** (www.myspace.com/rosiegarland) has three solo collections of poems and widely anthologised short stories and essays. Her first novel, *Animal Instinct*, is with her agent. She has an eclectic writing and performance history, from 80s Goth band 'The March Violets', to twisted cabaret as alter ego 'Rosie Lugosi the Vampire Queen' (www.rosielugosi.com). She's won the DaDa Award for Performance Artist of the Year and the Diva Award for Solo Performer.

**Claudia Van Gerven** says: I live in Boulder, Colorado, where I teach writing. My poems have been published in journals and magazines, including *Prairie Schooner*, *Calyx*, and *The Louisiana Review*, and appeared in numerous anthologies. I have received several national awards. Most recently, 'Octopus' was the Grand Prize winner in the 2008 Outrider Press Prize for poetry. Work of mine has been nominated for the Pushcart Prize. My chapbook, *The Ends of Sunbonnet Sue*, won the 1997 Angel Fish Press Prize and my full length manuscript, *The Spirit String*, has been a finalist in several national contests.

**Rebecca Goss** writes: Born in 1974, grew up in Suffolk, now lives in Liverpool. Pamphlet collection *Keeping Houston Time* by Slow Dancer Press. Poems in many magazines including *Stand*, *Ambit*, *Magma*, *Mslexia* and *Smiths Knoll*. MA in Creative Writing from Cardiff University. Maternal grandfather was Welsh and a number of relatives still live in South Wales. See www.poetrypf.co.uk

**Gabriel Griffin** writes: Childhood in Wales (family of Welsh origin), now lives on small island on Lake Orta, north Italy, Poems published in: *Scintilla*, *Peterloo*, *HQ*, *Poetry Life*, *Acorn*, *Still*, *White Adder*, *Leaf*, *Envoi* and others. Prized and placed in many competitions. Founder/organiser of *Poetry on the Lake* annual competition & festival (www.poetryonthelake.org)

**Trent Halliday** is a 28-year-old musician and poet born from the depths of Enfield's post-industrial bedrock. Since completing a degree in music at The City University, London, he has been working as a private guitar tutor, whilst becoming steadily more addicted to tea and verse. He currently resides in the fey wilds of Essex.

**Heather Harrison** is an exiled Geordie living in Worcestershire. A teacher and mum but always a writer, she had poems commissioned by Wolverhampton Art Gallery and West Midlands Arts who, with 'Common Ground', published her first poetry collection, *Roots Beneath the Pavement* (1987). During the 1980s, she also had poems, prose and children's stories broadcast by the BBC and published in small magazines. After more than a decade of working in classrooms, she now writes full time. In October 2004 she had three pieces performed at the RSC New Writing Festival; won the Seafield Publishing Poetry Competition in December 2005 and the Warwickshire Arts Festival Open Poetry Competition in July 2006. She has just completed her first full-length novel for children, *Magpie Runners*.

**Theresa Heine** says: I am an ex primary school teacher living in Mecklenburg, North Germany. My poems for children and adults appear in anthologies world wide. I have published two picture books with Barefoot Books.

**Emily Hinshelwood** says: As an anthropologist I've always been fascinated by the way stories are told, twisted and embroidered. I am drawn to interpretations and often find myself with several conflicting ones. Poetry, for me, is a way of mentally unknitting some of that confusion, and then reknitting it with my own needles. I'm a member of Merched y Wawr in Wales.

**Viki Holmes** is a widely anthologised and prize-winning British poet and performer who began her writing career in Cardiff as part of the Happy Demon poetry collective. She has been living and writing in Hong Kong since 2005. Her poetry has appeared in literary magazines and anthologies in Wales, England, Hong Kong, Australia, Canada, Macao and Singapore. She was twice a finalist in the John Tripp Award for Spoken Poetry (Wales), and was a runner-up in Hong Kong's inaugural Poetry Slam. Her first collection, *miss moon's class* is published by Chameleon Press (Hong Kong) and she is currently co-editing *Not A Muse*, a new anthology of women's writing that will be forthcoming in 2009 with Haven (Hong Kong).

**Marilyn Jenkins** says: I was born in Aberdare, educated in Aber and London, have been an English teacher, lecturer and adviser and am a member of the Welsh Academy. After travelling, I returned to Wales in 2000. My poetry has been published in *Anglo-Welsh Review; New Welsh Review; Paris Atlantic* and more recently in *Envoi*. My first collection, *Close Distances*, (supported by the Welsh Books Council) came out with Cinnamon in April 2007.

**Fred Johnston**: Born Belfast 1951. A reviewer, novelist and poet, he co-founded The Irish Writers' Co-operative in Dublin in the mid-Seventies and founded Galway's annual *Cúirt* Festival of Literature in 1986. He now manages the Western Writers' Centre there (www.twwc.ie). A translator, he has produced and published translation of contemporary French poems and stories and writes a good deal of his poetry in French nowadays as a personal, though possibly insignificant, protest against what has happened with much Irish poetry. He lives and works in Galway. *The Oracle Room*, his ninth collection of poetry, is published by Cinnamon Press.

**Dylan Jones** has published one full-length collection of poetry; *Dreaming Nightly of Dragons* (University of Salzburg 1996). He has contributed to a number of anthologies including; *The Poet's House* (Gomer 2000); *The Lie of the Land* (Cinnamon Press 2006) and *Only Connect* (Cinnamon Press 2007). He is a gardener, a self-taught artist, and singer with the folk-roots collective 'The Sheiling'.

**Wendy Klein** was born and brought up in the United States, but left forever in 1964. She has been writing poetry seriously for about seven years, and is a competition junkie who, to her intense surprise, has been published in a few magazines and has finally landed a collection—*Cuba in the Blood*, published in February 2009 by Cinnamon Press. She loves dogs, belly dancing and reading aloud. She hopes someone will destroy her humanely if she becomes too decrepit to manage all three. She takes her inspiration from everywhere, with a particular penchant for the family minefield.

**Gillian Laker** was born in Hong Kong and spent her childhood in a small village in Wiltshire. Her grandmother was Welsh. She now lives in Kent with her photographer husband and daughter. A number of her poems have appeared on the Guardian and Poets Against War websites and were shown as part of a multi-media exhibition held in Odense, Denmark.

**John Lehman** is the founder of *Rosebud*, a national magazine of short stories, poetry and illustration for people who enjoy good writing. He is also editor of the *Wisconsin People & Ideas*, co-editor of the free Madison/Milwaukee street-quarterly *Cup of Poems with a Side of Prose*, and originated the Prairie Fire Poetry Quartet. He teaches creative writing and acting techniques for writers in dozens of cities throughout the country. In 2005 he presented his first one-person play, *A Brief History of My Tattoo: Things I have Never Told Anyone Before*, at the Cornerstone Theatre in Milwaukee and in 2006 *The Jane Test: Ten Unexpected Encounters with Women* at the Overture Center in Madison. John lives with his wife and their four dogs in Wisconsin. His poetry books include: *Shrine of the Tooth Fairy; Dogs Dream of Running; Shorts: 101 Brief Poems of Wonder and Surprise* and *Acting Lessons*.

**Geoff Lowe** writes: a bits and pieces man. His stuff crops up in various places at odd times and in odd places at various other times. For many years he was founder-editor of *Psychopoetica*.

**Tamara Madison** has been writing ever since she could hold a pen; her work has appeared in various small press journals in the United States and the United Kingdom. Her chapbook *The Belly Remembers* won the Jane Buel Bradley Chapbook Award in 2005, and is published by Pearl Editions. Tamara teaches French in a no-longer-completely-failing high school in the Los Angeles Unified School District, and lives in Los Alamitos, California with her daughter and their vicious pit bull.

**Rachel Mann** says: I'm an Anglican priest based in south Manchester whose poetry has appeared in a range of magazines and anthologies. One day I hope to find the time to learn the piano.

**Jane McLaughlin** works in adult and further education and tries to find as much time for writing as she can. She has had poems published in numerous national magazines and anthologies and has been commended in several competitions. She regularly takes part in readings in London and elsewhere.

**Nicky Mesch** lives in Jersey. Her work has appeared in *Magma* as well as various anthologies, most recently *Outbox & Other Poems* (Leaf Books) and the *Channel Island Writers' Anthology 2008*.

**Kathy Miles** was born in Liverpool. She works as an Assistant Librarian at the University of Wales, Lampeter. She has published two books: *The Rocking-Stone* (Poetry Wales) and *The Third Day: Landscape and the Word*, (Gomer) and her work frequently appears in magazines and anthologies. She won the Ilkley Literature Poetry Festival 2008. Her latest collection, *The Shadow-House*, is published by Cinnamon Press in 2009.

**Helen Moore** is an ecopoet and children's author based near Bath. Helen publishes poetry, essays and reviews in various anthologies and journals, including *Green Spirit*, *Caduceus* and *Resurgence Magazine,* for which she has been guest poetry editor. Initiated as a Bard at Bedd Taliesin, Ceredigion, in 2004, Helen regularly performs her poetry around the UK. She also works as a sustainability educator, and as co-founder of the Green Arts Network and Bath Poetry Café. Her books include an illustrated nature journal, *Changing Nature,* (GreenSeer Books, 2006) and *Hope and the Magic Martian*, a short novel for 7-10s (Lollypop Publishing, 2008.) www.natures-words.co.uk.

**Susan Morgan** lives in Cardiff and works part-time in adult education. One of her courses takes place in the National Museum. Her short stories have been published by Honno and Blue Tattoo and she is working on a novel.

**Kristine Ong Muslim** writes: More than six hundred poems and stories by Kristine Ong Muslim have been published or are forthcoming in over two hundred journals and magazines worldwide. Her work has appeared in *Envoi, Iota, The Journal,* and *Cordite.*

**F.M. Nicholson** has been an award-winning teacher in an urban public high school for over 25 years, and a theater critic for Los Angeles suburban daily newspapers for over 30 years. She holds an MFA from Spalding University, and is the author of two books of poetry. Most recently, her work has appeared in *Pearl,* and been accepted for publication by the Santa Fe Writer's Project. Her chapbook, *Smoke and Mirrors* was a semi-finalist for the Robin Becker Chapbook Prize in 2008. She lives in Pasadena, California with her wife and fellow poet, her teenaged daughter, and an ancient cat.

**Helen Ogden** is a 28 year-old writer from Knaresborough, North Yorkshire. She has been previously published in *Orbis, Iota, Gold Dust* and *Goblin Fruit* although this is her first anthology.

**Ben Parker** says: I was born in Worcester in 1982 and recently graduated from UEA's Creative Writing MA. I have had poems published in a number of magazines including *iota* and *Agenda.*

**Helen Pizzey** holds an MA in Creative Writing from Bath Spa University College. She has had poems published in several UK anthologies and magazines, including *Mslexia* and *The Interpreter's House*, as well as *The Orange Coast Review* in America. Another of her poems has just been set for a large-scale choral and orchestral work commissioned under the Per Cent for Art Scheme in Ireland. Her short fiction appears in two anthologies published by Leaf Books. Helen is a member of the Stradling family, occupants of St Donat's Castle in Llantwit Major, Glamorgan from 1292-1738. St Donat's is now the home of the first of twelve United World Colleges, founded by Kurt Hahn to foster harmony and progress through international education.

**Seonad Plowman** writes: Living in the countryside has left me with an almost unhealthy obsession with nature, fairytales and the darkness within. I am also very interested in suburbia and its hidden depths. After studying Creative Writing and Film Studies at university, I am now working in a pathology lab which has enhanced my morbid fascination with all things inside the body, whether physical or mental.

**Susan Richardson** is a poet, performer and tutor of creative writing based in Wales. Her collection of poetry, *Creatures of the Intertidal Zone*, inspired by her journey through Iceland, Greenland and Newfoundland in the footsteps of an intrepid eleventh century female Viking, is published by Cinnamon Press. She regularly performs her work at literary festivals (including Hay and Cheltenham) and environmental events (including the Green Party conference) and is one of the resident poets on BBC Radio 4's 'Saturday Live'. She has held several writing residencies and run workshops in Finland, Australia and New Zealand as well as in the UK. Please visit: www.susanrichardsonwriter.co.uk and susanrichardsonwriter.blogspot.com

**Charles Ries** lives in Milwaukee, Wisconsin. His narrative poems, short stories, interviews and poetry reviews have appeared in over two hundred print and electronic publications. He is a founding member of the Lake Shore Surf Club, the oldest fresh water surfing club on the Great Lakes, and he is poetry editor for WORD RIOT (www.wordriot.org). You may find samples of his work by going to http://www.literati.net/Ries/

**Aleah Sato** is the author of *Badlands* and *Stillborn Wilderness* (Pooka Press 2008). Her work has appeared in *Nthposition, Adirondack Review, juked, Just West of Athens, Blue Fifth Review, Shadowtrain, BlazeVox, The Furnace Review, fourW 18, The Argotist,* and *Eclectica*, among others. Her collaboration with photographer, Elizabeth Siegfried, was recently exhibited at the G+ Galleries in Toronto.

**Lee-Anne Semple** says: I was born in Glasgow in 1973 but lived in Hong Kong until I was a teenager. I have spent the majority of my adult life in the North West of England working as airline cabin crew but recently successfully completed a degree in English Literature and Creative Writing at Salford University.

**Elizabeth Speller** says: I am an author, poet and journalist (from *The Big Issue* to the *Financial Times* to *Vogue*), and occasional university teacher, who lives in Gloucestershire and on a small Greek island. I have written four books and wrote the poem for this anthology while I held a Hosking Houses Trust Residency (for women writers). Currently I am writing about graveyards.

**Ed Taylor's** fiction and poetry have appeared in a number of US and UK journals. He lives in Buffalo, New York (USA).

**Pam Thompson** is a poet, lecturer and literature consultant living in Leicester. Pam has been widely published in magazines and anthologies and was a first stage prize winner in The Poetry Business pamphlet competition (2005). Her pamphlet, *Show Date and Time* was published in May, 2006. Former pamphlets are *Spin* (Waldean Press, 1999) and *Parting the Ghosts of Salt* (Redbeck Press, 2000). She has performed with a group of poets called Inky Fish; delivers writing workshops and has written to commission. She was a former winner of a writing bursary from East Midlands Arts and has undertaken several reading tours with other poets. Pam has a collection forthcoming from Redbeck Press.

**Bill Trüb** is a writer from coastal New Jersey. His poetry has been anthologized in *Your Messages* (2008) and *The Review of Contemporary Poetry* (2005), both published by bluechrome. Bill holds a Master's degree with distinction in creative writing from Cardiff University, and has performed his work in the UK and the US. He was poet-in-residence on a popular university radio show in Wales. Currently, he is the senior editor for a business magazine located near New York City. He is 26 years old.

**Ann Walters** lives in the Pacific Northwest. Her poetry has appeared in *Poetry International, Poet Lore, Orbis, Cadenza, The Pedestal Magazine,* and many others. She has been nominated for a Pushcart Prize and was a shortlist finalist in the *LICHEN* 2007 Tracking a Serial Poet competition.

**Martin Willitts Jr** has been in anthologies *Hurricane Blues, Primal Sanities, Mint Sauce and other stories and poems,* and *Allegheny River Anthology.* His recent book publications include *The Secret Language of the Universe* (March Street Press, 2006), *Lowering Nets of Light* (Pudding House Publications, 2007), *News from the Front* (www.slowtrains.com, 2007), *Alternatives to Surrender* (Plain View Press, 2007), *Words & Paper* (www.threelightsgallery.com 2008).

**Maria Wilson** is an artist whose video work uses narrative often involving anecdote or myth. She studied in Wales and has been resident there for the past 22 years. Her art work has been exhibited both internationally and locally. She has also run workshops and held residencies across South Wales. 'Persephone' is her first published poem. Maria is currently writing a screenplay with her sister.

**Sue Wood** lives in Halifax, West Yorkshire where she works as a freelance writer in health care and community settings. She has won or been placed in many national poetry competitions including a Cinnamon Press Poetry Collection Award. Her first collection *Imagine yourself to be water* is published by Cinnamon in April, 2009.